I0165212

Adventure on the Mountain

I Talk You Talk Press

Copyright © 2020 I Talk You Talk Press

ISBN: 978-4-909733-45-0

www.italkyoutalk.com

info@italkyoutalk.com

All rights reserved. No part of this publication may be resold, reproduced, stored in retrieval system, copied in any form or by any means, electronic, mechanical, photocopying, recording or otherwise transmitted without the prior written permission from the publisher. You must not circulate this publication in any format, online or otherwise.

This is a work of fiction. Names, characters, businesses, organizations, products, places, events and incidents are either the products of the author's imagination or are used in a fictitious manner. We have no affiliation with any existing companies mentioned in this story. Any resemblance to actual persons, living or dead, existing stories or actual events is purely coincidental.

Although the author and publisher have made every effort to ensure that the contents of this book were correct at press time, the author and publisher do not assume and hereby disclaim any liability to any party for any loss, damage, or disruption caused by errors or omissions, whether such errors or omissions result from negligence, accident, or any other cause.

For more information, see the Copyright Notice on our website.

Cover illustration image copyright: © ystewarthenderson #263928095 Adobe Stock Standard license

CONTENTS

I Talk You Talk Press

CHAPTER ONE

Junko and Hannah are friends. Junko is from Japan, and Hannah is from Germany. They study English at a language school in London. Now, they are travelling around the UK. They are in Scotland. They are going to climb a mountain today, so they get up early. They are staying in a small hotel near the mountain. The hotel owner, Gwen, is very friendly. Now, they are eating breakfast. Gwen is talking to them.

"Are you going to climb the mountain today?" asks Gwen.

"Yes," says Junko.

"Take care," says Gwen. "The weather is good now, but on the mountain, the weather changes very quickly."

"It's OK," says Hannah. "We have warm clothes, and lots of food and water in our backpacks."

"There is a hiking route on the mountain. Stay on the route. There are forests on the mountain. If you lose the route in the forest, you will get lost. A few years ago, a man climbed the mountain. He left the route in the forest to take some photographs. He got lost, and died on the mountain," says Gwen.

"We will stay on the route," says Junko.

"Be careful," says Gwen. "What time will you come back?"

"We will come back around three o'clock. We are going to have lunch at the top of the mountain," says Hannah.

Gwen goes into the kitchen. She comes back into the dining room with sandwiches.

"Here are some sandwiches for your lunch. Enjoy your day," says Gwen.

"Thank you!" say Junko and Hannah.

Junko and Hannah walk out of the dining room and go up to their room. They pack the sandwiches in their backpacks.

"Gwen is very kind," says Hannah.

"I think so too," says Junko. "We have sandwiches, meat pies, fruit, snacks and lots of chocolate. We have so much food!"

"And we have four bottles of water. My backpack is heavy!" says Hannah.

Junko and Hannah put their coats on and put their backpacks on their backs.

"OK! Time for an adventure!" says Hannah.

They walk out of their room and go down the stairs.

"See you later Gwen!" says Junko.

Gwen comes out of the dining room. "Have fun, and take care!" says Gwen.

CHAPTER TWO

Junko and Hannah walk to the mountain. It is a beautiful day. The sky is blue and there are no clouds.

"It is a good day to climb a mountain," says Hannah. "The view from the top of the mountain will be wonderful."

"I think so too," says Junko. "Look, here is a sign."

They read the sign ----*Hiking Route*----

"The hiking route starts here," says Junko. They start walking on the route. On both sides of the route there are many trees.

"The route goes through the forest," says Hannah. They walk on the route. After a few minutes, the route goes higher.

"We are climbing higher now," says Junko. She looks at her watch. "It is nine am. What time will we get to the top of the mountain?"

"About eleven o'clock," says Hannah. "At the top of the mountain we can take some photographs and relax. Let's eat lunch at around twelve o'clock, and then go back down the mountain."

"OK," says Junko.

It is quiet in the forest. There are no other people. They can hear birds singing.

"It is so peaceful here," says Junko.

"Yes, it's beautiful," says Hannah.

After thirty minutes, they come out of the forest. On each side of the route there is grass and there are large and small rocks. There are some rocks on the route.

"It is difficult to see the route," says Hannah. "There are so many rocks."

"And the route is not straight," says Junko. "It goes to the left and then to the right, and then to the left. We have to be careful."

"Oh look, here is another forest," says Hannah. They enter the next forest. It is dark in the forest. There are many tall trees, and they cannot see the sky.

"This forest is big," says Junko. "When we come out of the forest, we will be near the top of the mountain."

After thirty minutes, Hannah says, "Let's take a rest." They open their backpacks and take out some water and chocolate.

"This water tastes good," says Junko. "I'm thirsty."

"I'm thirsty too. It is cold on the mountain, but we are walking, so I feel hot," says Hannah. The put their water and chocolate back in their backpacks, and start walking again.

Junko looks at her watch. "We have been walking for one hour and thirty minutes," she says. "It takes two hours to climb this mountain. We are near the top."

They come out of the forest. They look at the sky. It is blue, but there are some clouds.

"It is getting cloudy," says Junko. "I hope it is not too cloudy at the top of the mountain. I want to take some pictures."

"I think it will be a little cloudy, but the clouds are high. We will have a good view," says Hannah.

They climb higher and higher. There are more rocks on the route. It is difficult to climb.

"I'm glad we have good hiking boots," says Junko.

"Me too," says Hannah. "These rocks are big."

"Look! The top of the mountain!" says Junko.

They climb up to the top.

"The view is great!" says Hannah. They put their backpacks down on the ground and take out their phones.

"Let's take a picture of us together!" says Junko. "When we return to the hotel, I'll post it on Instagram!"

They take many pictures. They can see other mountains, and they can see a small town and some small villages.

"The hotel is in that village over there," says Hannah.

The top of the mountain is flat. They walk around and take many photographs. They sit on the grass and relax. There are some clouds in the sky, but the sky is blue. It is a little cold at the top of the mountain, but Junko and Hannah have warm clothes. They feel warm.

Junko looks at the time. "It's twelve o'clock. Let's eat lunch," says Junko.

They take the sandwiches, pies, fruit and snacks out of their backpacks.

"The sandwiches from Gwen are really good," says Hannah. "I love cheese and tomato sandwiches."

They talk about their countries and their friends while they eat. Junko tells Hannah about life in Japan, and Hannah tells Junko about life in Germany. When they finish eating, they lie down and close their eyes. The sun is warm, and they feel sleepy. Hannah and Junko go to sleep.

CHAPTER THREE

"Junko! Wake up!" says Hannah.

Junko opens her eyes. "What?"

She looks at the sky. It is cloudy. She feels cold.

"I think it is going to rain," says Hannah. "We should go back to the hotel."

"I'm cold," says Junko. She puts on a hat. She looks up at the sky again. "The clouds are moving," she says. "They are moving lower."

"Let's go now," says Hannah.

They put their backpacks on their backs and start walking. The clouds move lower. Soon, it is very misty. They cannot see very clearly.

"I can't see the route," says Hannah.

"I can see it a little," says Junko. "But there are many rocks on the route and at the side of the route. Is this the route? I don't know."

"I can see the forest," says Hannah. "I think this is the route."

They walk into the forest.

"Hannah, I can't see the route," says Junko. They look at the ground carefully. They can see grass and rocks, but no route.

"Let's go back," says Hannah. "Let's get out of the forest. It is so dark in here. Maybe we can find the route outside the forest. We entered the forest five minutes ago."

They turn around and start to climb the mountain again. They climb for fifteen minutes, but they don't leave the forest.

"We are lost," says Hannah.

"What are we going to do?" asks Junko.

"I don't know," says Hannah.

Then it starts raining. The rain in the dark forest is noisy. They put their backpacks on the ground and take out their raincoats. They put their raincoats on.

"Maybe we can call someone to help us," says Junko. They look at their phones.

"We have no signal. We can't use our phones," says Hannah. They look at each other.

"Let's walk down the mountain," says Junko. "Maybe we will find the route again. Or maybe there is another route."

"OK," says Hannah. They start walking again.

CHAPTER FOUR

An hour later, they are still in the forest. It is very dark and wet. It is raining heavily.

"We are lost," says Hannah. "And very wet." She looks at her phone. "It is four pm. Gwen will be worried. Maybe she will call the police."

"What's that?" asks Junko.

"What?" asks Hannah.

"Over there. It looks like a building."

"A building?" Hannah looks through the trees. "Yes, you are right. It looks like a building."

They walk to the building. It is small. It is made of wood. There is only one room in the building.

"Why is there a building here?" asks Hannah.

"I don't know. Maybe it is a rest place for hikers," says Junko. "Let's look inside."

They open the door slowly. It is very dark inside, so they use the light from their phones to look around.

"Look at this!" says Junko. "There are some clothes. There is a small backpack."

"Maybe a hiker forgot to take them," says Hannah. "What is in the backpack?"

They look in the backpack.

"There are some snacks, and some clothes," says Junko. "And a lot of money."

"What are you doing here?" says a man's voice.

Junko and Hannah turn around and look at the door. There is a man. He is tall and has long hair. He is wearing dirty clothes. He looks around forty years old.

Hannah and Junko feel very scared.

"I'm sorry. We got lost," says Junko. "We will go now."

The man looks at them.

"You are very far from the hiking route. It is raining. It is misty. It is very cold. It is dark. You won't find the route."

"What should we do?" asks Hannah.

The man says, "You can stay here tonight. Tomorrow, when it is light, I will take you to the route."

"Thank you," says Hannah. "But, I have a question. Do you live here?"

The man looks at Hannah. "Don't ask me any questions," he says angrily.

"I'm sorry," says Hannah.

"Sit down," says the man. They sit down.

"Do you have any food?" asks the man.

"Yes, we have food," says Junko. "Are you hungry?"

"Yes," says the man. Junko and Hannah take out their snacks and chocolate. They give some to the man. He takes them and eats quickly.

"What do you usually eat?" asks Junko.

"No questions!" says the man loudly.

"Sorry," says Junko.

"It is cold. I am going to build a fire outside," says the man.

"But it is wet," says Hannah.

"There is a dry area at the back of this building. There are many trees, so the rain doesn't fall there." The man takes a lighter out of his backpack and goes out.

Junko and Hannah look at each other. "Who is he?" asks Hannah quietly. "And why is he here?"

"I don't know," says Junko. "Maybe he lives on the mountain. It's strange."

A few minutes later, the man comes back.

"I made a fire," he says, "Come outside. It is warm near the fire."

Junko and Hannah go outside. There is a small fire near the building. They sit down.

"It is very warm," says Junko. The man sits next to them.

"Where are you from?" asks the man.

"I'm from Japan," says Junko.

"And I'm from Germany," says Hannah. "We are students at a language school in London. We are visiting Scotland for a few days. We are staying in a hotel in the village near here."

The man says, "Tomorrow, when you go back into the village, don't tell anyone about me. OK?"

"OK," say Junko and Hannah.

"Promise?" asks the man.

"We promise," say Junko and Hannah.

Junko and Hannah look at each other. *Who is this man? And why is he here?*

CHAPTER FIVE

It is late at night. Junko, Hannah and the man go into the building. They use the light from their mobile phones.

"You can sleep over there," says the man. "I will sleep here."

The man has two blankets. He gives one blanket to Hannah and Junko. The two young women lie down together. The floor is hard, and it is cold. But it is warmer than outside.

The man lies down on the floor. Soon, he is asleep.

"Junko," says Hannah quietly. "Are you awake?"

"Yes, I am," says Junko. "I can't sleep. The floor is very hard."

"Do you think the man is dangerous?" asks Hannah.

"I don't know," says Junko.

"I can't sleep," says Hannah. "There is a strange man in the room. I feel it is dangerous."

"He is sleeping. Maybe it is OK," says Junko.

A few minutes later, the young women go to sleep.

The next morning, Junko and Hannah wake up at 5:00am. It is dark outside.

"Where is the man?" asks Hannah. "He isn't here."

Junko looks around the room. "I don't know. But we should get up."

The two young women get up.

"Did you sleep OK?" asks Junko.

"Yes. I was tired," says Hannah. "How about you?"

"I was tired, too. But I woke up many times in the night," says

Junko.

"We have to find the route," says Hannah. "I think Gwen is worried about us. I think she called the police. I think people are searching for us."

"I think so, too," says Junko.

The door opens and the man comes in. He is carrying some plants and berries.

"Breakfast," he says. He gives Junko and Hannah some plants and berries. The young women look at them.

"Are these safe to eat?" asks Hannah.

The man smiles. "Yes, they are. I eat them every day."

The man sits down, and they eat the plants and berries together. They taste very bad, but Hannah and Junko are hungry.

"Thank you," says Junko. "Can you take us to the route now?"

"Yes, I'll take you to the route now. Come on," says the man.

Hannah and Junko pick up their backpacks and go outside with the man.

The man walks quickly. They walk through the forest. It is cold and dark, but it is not raining. They walk for thirty minutes. Then, the man stops.

"Here is the route," he says.

"Thank you very much," say Hannah and Junko.

"Remember, don't tell anyone about me," says the man.

"We won't tell anyone," says Hannah.

The man goes back into the forest. Hannah and Junko watch him.

"He is very strange," says Junko. "But he helped us."

The young women start to walk down the mountain route quickly.

CHAPTER SIX

"Hannah! Junko! I was so worried about you!" says Gwen. "I called the police. Yesterday, the police and volunteers looked for you on the mountain. But the weather was very bad, so they gave up. They planned to start looking again this morning. I will call the police now."

Junko and Hannah are back at the hotel. They are sitting in the warm dining room. Gwen calls the police and comes back into the room.

"I will make you a big breakfast," she says. She goes into the kitchen. A few minutes later, she comes back with two plates of eggs, bacon, sausages, mushrooms and toast. She brings a large pot of coffee and some water.

She watches Junko and Hannah eat. They eat quickly because they are hungry. She sits down at the next table.

"What did you eat? What did you drink? Where did you sleep?" Gwen asks many questions.

"We ate our pies, snacks and chocolate. We drank our water," says Junko.

"We slept in…." Hannah stops. She looks at Junko. "We slept in the forest," she says.

"Was it cold?" asks Gwen.

"Yes, it was cold, but we were OK," says Junko.

A policeman walks into the room. "You are safe," he says. He sits down, and Gwen gives him a cup of coffee. "We searched for you yesterday, but the weather was too bad. You look fine. I am surprised.

It was very cold last night on the mountain. It was raining. Why are you OK?"

"We had extra clothes in our backpacks, and we had snacks and water," says Junko.

"But where did you sleep?" asks the policeman.

"In the forest," says Hannah. "It was cold, but we were OK."

The policeman asks them more questions. Hannah and Junko do not tell him about the man or the building.

When the policeman goes, the young women go up to their rooms. They are very tired.

"I want to sleep all day," says Junko.

"Me too," says Hannah.

They take a shower, and go to bed.

CHAPTER SEVEN

Hannah and Junko sleep all day. They wake up in the evening, and Gwen makes them some dinner. Then, they go to bed again. They wake up the next morning. They feel better. After breakfast, they go for a walk in the village. The village is small. There is a post office, a bank, a supermarket and a few other shops. It is cold and raining.

Some people say to them, "Are you the hikers on the mountain? We were worried about you!"

"I want to buy a drink and some snacks. Let's go into that small supermarket," says Junko. They walk into the supermarket. They buy some drinks and snacks. They walk out of the supermarket. Then Hannah stops.

"Junko, look." She points to a poster in the window. Junko looks at the poster. On the poster, there is a photograph of a man. They read the poster carefully.

"This man robbed a shop in the next village. He had a knife. He went into the shop and said, 'Give me the money.' He is a very dangerous man. The police are looking for him," says Junko.

"Look at the picture" says Hannah. "He looks like someone. He looks like…"

The young women look at each other.

"He looks like the man on the mountain," says Hannah.

They are very shocked. "What should we do?" asks Junko.

"We said to the man, 'We won't tell anyone about you,'. We promised. And he helped us. The mountain was very dangerous. It was cold and raining. He saved our lives," says Hannah.

"But he is a bad man," says Junko. "We have to tell the police."

"I think so too," says Hannah. "But it is difficult. I feel bad."

"Let's think about it," says Junko.

They go back to the hotel and sit on their beds.

"What do you think?" asks Hannah.

"The man had a knife. He took a lot of money. We have to tell the police," says Junko.

"You are right. We have to tell the police," says Hannah. She stands up. "Come on, let's go and talk to Gwen.

They go downstairs. Gwen is cleaning the dining room.

"Gwen, can we talk to you?" asks Junko.

"Of course!" says Gwen.

"It's about the mountain. We didn't tell you everything yesterday." They sit down.

"Please tell me," says Gwen.

"On the mountain, we got lost. We couldn't find the route. We saw an old building in the forest. We went inside the building. Then, a man came into the building."

"A man?" Gwen is surprised. "Was he hiking on the mountain too?"

"No," says Hannah. "He was staying on the mountain. He was staying in the building."

"Staying in the building? That is strange," says Gwen.

"He made a fire, and he said, 'You can sleep in the building,'" says Junko. "And in the morning, he gave us plants and berries for breakfast."

"When we went to the supermarket, we saw a poster. A man took a knife to a shop and took some money."

"Yes, it happened in the next village a few weeks ago. It was very bad," says Gwen.

"Well, this is difficult to say, but the man in the photograph is the man on the mountain," says Hannah.

"What?" Gwen is very surprised. She stands up quickly. "We have to call the police! Why didn't you tell me and the policeman yesterday?"

"Because the man helped us. He said, 'Don't tell anyone about me.' So, we didn't tell you," says Junko.

Gwen picks up her phone and calls the police. A policeman and a policewoman come. They ask Junko and Hannah many questions.

"We will search for the man now," says the policeman. "When are you going back to London?"

"We are going back tomorrow," says Junko.

"You can't go back," says the policeman. "When we find the man, you can go back."

"But we have English classes. They start the day after tomorrow," says Hannah.

"I'm sorry," says the policeman. "This is more important than your English classes!"

CHATPER EIGHT

Junko and Hannah stay in the hotel that day. It is cold and rainy, and they don't want to go out. They are worried. Will the police find the man?

The next evening, the policeman and a policewoman come to the hotel.

They sit down in the lobby with Gwen, Junko and Hannah.

"Did you find the man?" asks Hannah.

"Yes, we found the man," says the policeman.

"Is he OK?" asks Junko.

The policeman and policewoman look at each other. "He is dead," says the policeman.

"Dead? But, why? How?" Junko and Hannah are very surprised.

"We found him in the forest. He wasn't near the building. We think he was trying to escape. Maybe he thought, 'The women will tell someone about me. The police will find me. I have to go.' So, he walked through the forest at night. He fell over. He broke his leg. He couldn't move. It was very cold and wet in the forest. He died because he was cold and wet. We checked his backpack. He had a knife and a lot of money," says the policewoman.

"But why did he stay on the mountain?" asks Junko.

"Because it is a good place to hide. We found his name. He is from the big town near here."

"But he knew the mountain very well. He knew the place of the route. How did he know?" asks Junko.

"He is from this village. He moved to the big town when he was eighteen years old. His mother and father died. All the people in the village know the route, and the building. Maybe he played on the mountain when he was a child," says the policeman.

"Did he plan to stay on the mountain for a long time?" asks Hannah.

"We don't know. Maybe he thought, 'If I stay on this mountain for a few weeks, people will forget about the shop and the money.' So I think he was waiting," says the policewoman.

"I have a question," says Junko. "When did he die?"

"We think he died yesterday," says the policewoman.

Junko and Hannah look at each other.

"We didn't tell you about the man. So, you didn't look for him. Then, he died," says Junko. "I'm sorry. He saved our lives. But we couldn't save his life."

Junko and Hannah feel bad.

"But the man said, 'Don't tell anyone'. So you didn't tell anyone. You did a good thing," says Gwen.

"I don't know," says Hannah. "I think we did a bad thing. We didn't tell you about the man. Now, the man is dead."

The policeman and policewoman ask some more questions. Then, the policeman says, "You can go back to London tomorrow."

The next day, Junko and Hannah say goodbye to Gwen. They take the train back to London. They don't tell people about the mountain or the man. They feel bad and want to forget about it. They study hard. The adventure on the mountain is their secret.

THANK YOU

Thank you for reading Adventure on the Mountain. We hope you enjoyed the story. (Word count: 4,054)

There are quizzes about this book on our free study site I Talk You Talk Press EXTRA. http://italk-youtalk.com

If you would like to read more graded readers, please visit our website http://www.italkyoutalk.com

Other Level 1 graded readers include
A Business Trip to New York
A Homestay in Auckland
A Trip to London
Dear Ellen
Emily's Bag
Haruna's Story Part 1
Haruna's Story Part 2
Haruna's Story Part 3
Jimmy Luther
Ken's Story Part 1
Ken's Story Part 2
Life is Surprising!
Strange Stories
The Christmas Present
The Old Hospital

Wei's Part Time Job
We Met Online

ABOUT THE AUTHOR

I Talk You Talk Press is an award-winning Japan-based publisher of language textbooks, graded readers and language learning/teaching resources.

Our team is made up of highly experienced language teachers and translators, who have all studied at least one additional language to an advanced level.

This experience enables us to design our materials from the perspective of both the teacher and the learner. We consult with both teachers and language learners when designing our textbooks and graded readers, and test our materials extensively in the classroom before publication.

We are a fast-growing press, and currently publish graded readers for learners of English. We publish new graded readers monthly.

www.ingramcontent.com/pod-product-compliance
Lightning Source LLC
Chambersburg PA
CBHW022352040426
42449CB00006B/843